Contents

Friends of the Cromford Canal

The Friends of the Cromford Canal is an organisation whose aim is
to promote the restoration to navigation of the Cromford Canal,
its connection to the national waterways system, and the conservation, use,
maintenance and development of all its features, for the public benefit.

Chairman: Mike Kelley 01773 833425
Membership Secretary: Yvonne Shattower 0115 946 4479

Visit www.cromfordcanal.org.uk for more information including both historic and
present day photographs and membership form

FRONT COVER:- Langley Bridge Lock No.14 and Junction of the Cromford and
Nottingham Canals at Langley Mill.
BACK COVER:- Cromford Wharf after the first FCC Sponsored Walk in Sept. 2002

Published 2003 by the Friends of the Cromford Canal
© Written and compiled by Michael Harrison & Valerie Roberts
Centre spread map: Hugh Potter
All uncredited photographs by the authors

ISBN 0-9544482-0-0

All proceeds from the sale of this booklet will be used
to further the aims of the Friends of the Cromford Canal

Foreword

by Mike Kelley, Chairman,
Friends of the Cromford Canal

Welcome to the Walker's Guide to the Cromford Canal. This once busy waterway is not only rich in history, it also crosses some of the most beautiful countryside in the Midlands. This book will guide your steps through this countryside, while at the same time pointing out the sights of this considerably rich historical area.

The main line of the canal is currently in three distinct sections. Each section is within this booklet and can be taken as a separate walk, although the fit walkers among you may want to cover the whole 15 miles in one go. For the rest, each section is taken as an individual walk of between four and six miles.

The first walk is the southern section and goes from Langley Mill to Ironville and crosses open meadows and the nature reserves of the Brinsley Flash wetlands, then gradually climbs the old, and unfortunately now derelict, flight of seven locks, up to the junction with the 2 mile Pinxton Branch which is described separately. Just beyond the junction is the Codnor Park Reservoir, an attractive area of open water and full of wildlife.

The second walk is the central section and covers an amazing variety of countryside. Starting in the Golden Valley, crossing over the Butterley tunnel, one of the longest canal tunnels in the country, later the canal walk becomes elevated high above the rooftops of the local houses.

The third, the northern section, is the most well known part of the canal. At the start of this walk an attractive detour, giving extensive views over the Amber Valley, is required to by-pass two industrial sites that were built on the line of the canal. Once this is traversed the Derwent Valley is reached and is followed all the way to the terminus of the canal at Cromford Wharf. There are splendid views across the valley and areas are seen that were in the forefront of the Industrial Revolution. So much so, that the United Nations has declared the mills of the Derwent Valley to be a World Heritage Site.

Enjoy your walks and at the same time help us to preserve the Cromford Canal for future generations.

Cromford Canal
Langley Mill to Codr

The Cromford Canal begins at Langley Mill where it joins the Erewash Canal below the A608 Bridge No. 49. Langley Bridge Lock No. 14, the only operable one on the canal, is immediately above the bridge. This lock was restored from a derelict condition by volunteer members of the Erewash Canal Preservation &

The junction with the Erewash Canal below Bridge No. 49

Development Association and re-opened to navigation in May 1973.

Just above here, the derelict Nottingham Canal makes a junction with the Cromford. The swing bridge and stop lock at the entrance to this canal, giving access to the Great Northern Basin, were restored at the same time. The Great Northern Inn adjoins the basin. Note also the former Nottingham Canal toll house beyond the swing bridge.

Langley Bridge Lock No. 14

Langley Mill Boatyard's dry dock, workshop and moorings now occupy the first length of the Cromford Canal above the junction. The towpath passes through the boatyard, but terminates at their top boundary. It was diverted when the area was opencast mined. Beyond the boatyard the A610 bypass road crosses the canal line shortly above the site of Strutts Lock No.13. To start this walk we must therefore, for the time being, make a diversion as follows:

From the lock, walk along the main road towards Langley Mill passing the Esso station, over the River Erewash bridge and turn right along a signed footpath, just before The Mill public house. Follow this path behind Smith's flour mill, and continue along the left side of the river (do not cross the footbridge). Pass a weir on the river and then follow the path which turns left round the corner of an asbestos building and continue to meet Cromford Road, opposite Argyle Street.

Turn right along Cromford Road and continue past the Durham Ox public house. As Cromford Road bends to the left, keep straight on along Plumptre Road. At the end, take the track straight ahead to the left of Plumptre farmhouse.

Pass under the A610 bypass bridge (the railway is on your left) and follow the track round to the right (NOT the footpath straight ahead). Continue along this track, which is Stoney Lane, for some 400 yards and re-cross River Erewash on a low level bridge. After a further 150 yards is the site of Stoney Lane Bridge No. 45 over the canal and just beyond, a public footpath to Brinsley Hill and Jacksdale is signed to the left.

Turn left along this signed footpath which is to the right of the actual canal line, but follows it closely. Beyond, a small copse on the left of the path is the site of Vickers Lock No.12. It is not readily accessible, but the determined walker can scramble into the undergrowth where traces of the lock chamber top coping stones can be found. Further to the left the flashes on the River Erewash caused by mining subsidence can be seen.

Pass over a stile straight ahead into a second field and follow the path, then over another stile into a third field, and continue straight ahead keeping to the left of the hedge. You are now on the canal line. Shortly fork left at a stile (do not pass over this one) and continue, to cross a footbridge over the river. This is the site of the River Erewash aqueduct. Some remains of the brickwork of the aqueduct can be seen in the river to the right of the footbridge.

Follow the footpath across the field ahead, then over a double stile into the next one. There are no traces of the two Stoneyford Locks, Nos. 11 & 10, which were in this length. Another double stile then and across a third field to pass close to the right of a small red brick cottage, now part of a boarding kennels. This is the site of Boat Lane Bridge No. 41. The bridge was immediately adjacent to the cottage which was near the water's edge.

Cottage beside site of Boat Lane Bridge No 41

Those wanting refreshment at this stage can visit Stoneyford Lodge, formerly the Boat Inn, which is up the track beyond the railway bridge.

Walkers queuing to pass the stile into the Derbyshire Wildlife Trust Section

Carry straight on, with the kennels on your left, over another stile and into the section of the canal line now owned by the Derbyshire Wildlife Trust. Some remains of canalside stone wall are visible in the hedgerow on the left. Stoneyford Top Lock No. 9 was shortly above here, but again there is no trace nowadays. This whole area has not only suffered from deep mine subsidence, but the entire landscape has been altered by opencast coal workings. Brinsley Flash is on the right.

4

Pass another stile, noting yellow arrows and continue along the path to the right of the hedge. We are still on the canal line here. The next stile is by the site of Slaley's Bridge No. 40. Butterley Company Lock No. 8 was shortly above here.

Pass straight on at the junction where another footpath goes off to the left and continue ahead past an interpretation board about Erewash Meadows Nature Reserve, then to the remains of a railway bridge. Just here, pass over a stile and cross to the right over some running water via a small footbridge and continue ahead.

The reed filled canal bed, with a good towpath on the right, is now easily followed. This is the first length of obvious canal since leaving Langley Mill. The Forge opencast coal site to the left of the canal is now apparent. A concrete weir across the canal line now retains water at a higher level. We shortly come to the junction bridge which marks the entrance to the former Portland Basin on the right. This was a short branch of the canal which led to Jacksdale Wharf.

Pass over this bridge and immediately through the remains of a railway bridge. Beyond here, there are a few signs of the Butterley Old Forge buildings adjoining the canal on the left bank.

Remains of Codnor Park Maintenance Yard

We now reach Lock No. 7, the first of the Codnor Park flight. Continue up to Marshall's Lock No. 6 where the remains of a narrow dry dock can be seen alongside the lock chamber. Above here on the towpath side are the former canal maintenance yard and

Restoration Project at Codnor Park

stables. These buildings were intact until a few years ago, but they have now fallen into dereliction. However, the stone cottage

which is part of this interesting complex is now being restored.

This is shortly followed by Gas House Lock No.5. Although all of these locks are overgrown and partially filled with rubbish, the stone lock chambers are mostly intact and are still in a reasonable condition, but the lock gates have long since rotted away and disappeared.

Gas House Lock No 5

After this lock is the bridge (No. 38) carrying the main Erewash Valley railway line. The canal passes through the left of the two arches and immediately into Smith's Lock No. 4.

Here can be seen the remains of the anchor bracket which held the bottom lock gate into its pivot point in the quoin stone.

Note also, in the bottom gate recess, a deep groove caused by the ropes from the thousands of horse drawn boats which have passed this way. It is difficult to imagine now the large volume of traffic which formerly used this waterway.

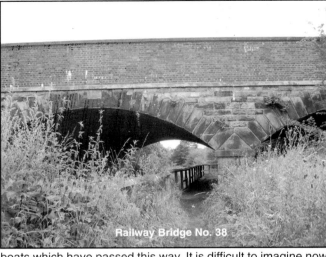
Railway Bridge No. 38

Bottom Gate Anchor

Rope Wear on the Coping Stone

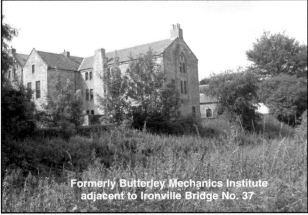
Formerly Butterley Mechanics Institute adjacent to Ironville Bridge No. 37

Continue up into Ironville, an interesting village built by the Butterley Company for its workers. Adjacent to the towpath there are stone buildings now used by a road transport firm. On the opposite side of the canal is another impressive stone building. This was formerly the Butterley Company Mechanics Institute, later the Forge offices, now converted into attractive apartments.

This is followed by Ironville Bridge No. 37, a fine stone arch in original condition at the tail of Pottery Lock No. 3.

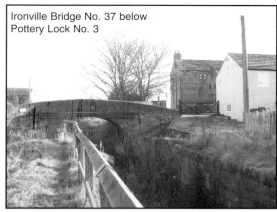
Ironville Bridge No. 37 below Pottery Lock No. 3

Another short pound leads to a second stone arch bridge (No. 36) below Boat Dock Lock No. 2. Note the iron guards on the bridge abutments. These were to protect the stonework from the wear caused by the towlines from the horse drawn boats, very necessary looking at the grooves worn in them.

Above this lock the canal channel has been deepened. There is now no sign of the Top Lock No. 1, which was obliterated and the site excavated in the 1980s. This was deemed necessary at the time to provide a flood relief channel for the adjacent Codnor Park reservoir. The level of the reservoir was also lowered and the large overflow weir constructed at the same time.

Top Lock Bridge No. 1, Codnor Park. Site of former junction with the Pinxton Branch

Here also is the junction with the Pinxton Branch which leaves to the right. The walk along this branch is well worth doing and is described later in this guide. The bridge at the entrance carrying the main line towpath is another intact stone arch bridge.

Pass by this bridge and continue across the footbridge over the reservoir overflow to a small car park on the infilled canal line.

This car park is convenient for those arranging return transport.

A catering van provides excellent hot food and drinks here, as well as limited toilet facilities.

Codnor Park Reservoir and new footbridge over relief channel leading to the car park

Cromford Canal Walk : Stage 2
Codnor Park to Bullbridge - 5 miles

Starting from the car park on the canal line at the eastern end of Codnor Park Reservoir, the towpath passes between the reservoir on the right and the infilled canal on the left. On leaving the car park, notice a quoin stone from the top lock beside the path. Follow the path to the far end of the reservoir, cross the footbridge then keep left to continue on the towpath towards Golden Valley.

Site of Golden Valley Bridge No. 34

Note the concrete milepost on the towpath, showing $10^{1}/2$ miles to Cromford. Carry on under the derelict Footbridge No. 35 to the site of Golden Valley Bridge No. 34. Walk up the slope and cross the road to the Newlands Inn. Food is available here.

Take care when crossing the road

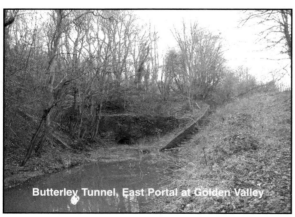

Butterley Tunnel, East Portal at Golden Valley

Follow the path down the left of the pub and along the towpath to see the eastern portal of Butterley Tunnel. Retrace your steps a short way and turn left up the bank to the narrow gauge Newlands Inn railway station. See page 16 for details of the Midland Railway Centre. Alternatively, the station can be reached directly by walking round the back of the Newlands Inn from the car park.

Over Butterley Tunnel

Having looked at the eastern portal of Butterley Tunnel and the narrow gauge railway station behind the Newlands Inn, retrace your steps to the road. Turn right and pass over the canal line at the site of Golden Valley Bridge No. 34, then take the first turn right on to Coach Road. This is a former toll road which ran through the Butterley Estate and closely follows the line of the tunnel. The road is still private and vehicular use is restricted, but there is a public footpath along it.

Walk straight up the road passing Spinney Lodge Guest House and a turn to the right. Pass several "Private Road" signs and on to the old toll bar. There is a gate across at this point, beside a terrace of cottages and a farm. Pass over the stile to the left of the gate, and continue along the road. Note on the left here, the first of the ventilation shafts for the tunnel.

This is a brick chimney - like structure in the centre of a mound of earth which was made from the spoil drawn up the shaft

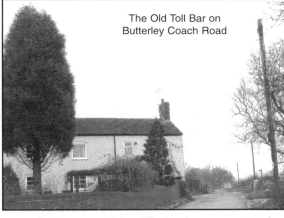

The Old Toll Bar on Butterley Coach Road

when the tunnel was being constructed. The mound is still clearly apparent today, although long since grassed over.

Butterley Tunnel ventilation shaft

A little further on is another vent on the right hand side, although this one is nowadays a rectangular concrete structure. Continuing along the road, there is a bridge over a derelict railway and after this a turn to the right, which leads to the Derbyshire Police helicopter unit and vehicle workshops. Again carry straight on passing a turn to the left with an attractive former Butterley Estate Lodge House on the corner. In a short distance the Headquarters of Derbyshire Constabulary at Butterley Hall is seen on the left, so please be on your best behaviour! On the right opposite this is a third tunnel vent standing on another mound covered in trees. This one is brick built and still retains the hemispherical iron grille on the top.

Follow the road then round to the right,

past an entrance to Butterley Engineering and over two un-gated level crossings for their private railway. The road has now re-crossed the line of the tunnel which passes directly under the Butterley Works. Continue down the road with the works on the left, until reaching the Ripley to Alfreton road, adjacent to the Butterley Company's main entrance.

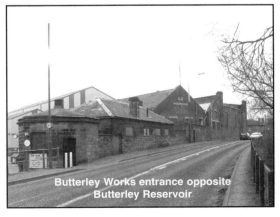

Butterley Works entrance opposite Butterley Reservoir

The Butterley reservoir, which supplied the canal, is immediately opposite. Cross the main road and turn left, noting the historic blue British Waterways sign for the reservoir, pictured on the right. Just before the sharp bend in the road, known locally as Butterley Corner, turn right down a track passing to the left of Lakeside Motors, and follow this track along the south side of the reservoir. Shortly

turn right on to a footpath alongside the western end. There is also a white 1970s style British Waterways notice here, again confirming that this is Butterley Reservoir.

Footpath crossing at Hammersmith Station

At the end of this path, cross a small bridge over the reservoir overflow and over a stile. Continue ahead through a small car park, over a second stile to gain access to Hammersmith Station. This is the western terminus of the preserved railway operated by the Midland Railway Centre. Cross straight over the track via the boardwalk at the end of the platform.

Beware of occasional steam trains [*See also Page 16*]

Over another stile and turn left along a footpath at the back of the station platform. This path becomes a track which joins the road at the bottom of the hamlet of Hammersmith. Cross the road and turn right under the adjacent A38 bridge. Immediately through the bridge, turn left on to a signed public footpath, which passes to the left of Geeson's scrapyard.

The first FCC sponsored walk following the footpath by Hammersmith Station

Continue down this path and, keeping left at the fork, drop down to join the towpath. Look back to see the western portal of Butterley Tunnel. The actual tunnel portal is hidden by a modern culvert which was installed to lengthen the tunnel when the A38 was built over this end.

Follow the overgrown towpath on the right of the canal channel to the A610 embankment. Pass up a few steps and over a stile, then up a long flight of steps to the A610 trunk road. Turn right for 40 yards along the pavement to a step, then stride over the crash barrier and cross the road.

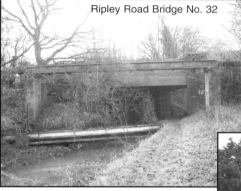
Western Portal of Butterley Tunnel

Ripley Road Bridge No. 32

Beware of fast moving traffic!

Pass down a similar staircase on the other side to rejoin the towpath, which is now easily followed. On to the modern Ripley Road Bridge No. 32 and pass under on the towpath. Food is available from the Gate Inn which is adjacent to this bridge.

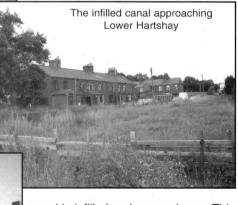
The infilled canal approaching Lower Hartshay

Follow what is now a good towpath with a concrete edge to Lower Hartshay village.

The apparent channel finishes here at a fence across the canal with a stile for the towpath, beyond which the

Looking back to site of Hartshay Bridge No. 31 marked by arched pipe at Lower Hartshay

canal is infilled and grassed over. This short length is used for grazing horses.

Following the towpath to the right of this section, a second stile brings us to Bridle Lane and the site of Hartshay Bridge No. 31, now destroyed. Note the green pipe which is still arched where it crossed the canal adjacent to the bridge.

Cross the lane and carry on along the signed footpath in front of the cottages, by the infilled bed. Pass over a stile and follow the footpath directly across two fields with no sign of the canal.

Part way across the second field, turn left at the hedge to follow the signed footpath. Pass over a stile close to the hedge to join the towpath and visible water channel just before Stavern's or Starvehimvalley Bridge No. 29, which is an intact original stone arch bridge.

From Bridle Lane the footpath is signed along the front of these cottages

Beyond this bridge the channel has been widened to form a fishing lake, with the towpath on the right. Then the canal is again infilled and the path crosses the line to the left bank and joins a track, which continues on the left of the canal line until the rear car park of The Excavator public house is reached.

Starvehimvalley Bridge No. 29

Pass under the Railway Bridge No. 28, round to the left and carry on through the front car park. This is on the line of the canal.

Line of canal under Railway Bridge No. 28 passes through car park of the Excavator Inn

Just beyond the car park is the short Buckland Hollow tunnel which is cut through solid rock. The canal channel through the tunnel is infilled, but one can walk through on the towpath.

Buckland Hollow Tunnel

Gardens extended over canal bed at Sawmills

The path now continues on the infilled canal bed and then on the towpath to the right of the channel. There is a stone wall between the towpath and the A610 through Sawmills which is on a much lower level than the canal at this point. There are then several allotments with various greenhouses and sheds etc. on the canal line, but the public footpath is intact.

The entrance to Lockwood's Works cuts through the canal embankment

Just after this, a section of the embankment has been removed where Lockwood's entrance road cuts across the line of the canal at main road level. Pass down the steps, across Lockwood's road and straight on up the track opposite and under the right hand arch of the stone Sawmills Bridge No. 26, to rejoin the canal.

The channel beyond this bridge is very overgrown but the towpath is easily followed. Continue until a signed junction is reached indicating a turn to the right just before a stone cottage.

Sawmills Bridge No. 26

Stone Chapel at the site of Bullbridge Aqueduct

Turn right here, down the steps to the A610, and emerge from behind an old stone chapel. This is the site of Bullbridge Aqueduct.

Cross directly over the road and straight ahead to the railway line. Climb over the stile and cross the railway via the boardwalk. A footbridge is due to be built here shortly, but in the meantime, **please take care as trains pass here at 100mph !**

High above Drover's Way

Over the stile beyond the railway, take the left hand fork of the path and up the steps to canal level. Continue to a wooden fence across the canal bed, over another stile and follow the towpath on the left of the canal line. Look over the wall to your left to see Drover's Way passing under the canal far below. This part of the aqueduct is still intact.

The path now passes to the left of a bungalow which has been built on the canal line.

After this the canal is in water as far as Bull Bridge No. 19, near to the Canal Inn. Although filled in, this bridge is intact.

This is the end of the second section of the walk.

Bull Bridge No. 19

The Midland Railway - Butterley

by Alan Calladine

The route of the Midland Railway-Butterley line parallels the Cromford Canal from Ironville through to the western end of Butterley tunnel where it too is blocked by the A38. The original Midland Railway Company bought out the Cromford Canal and following its tradition the Railway Museum also owns a short length of canal from the Newlands Inn to the Butterley Tunnel eastern portal.

Walking up the canal from Ironville you will see the railway line higher up the valley on the right hand side and may see some passing trains. By climbing the steps in the cutting just beyond the Newlands Inn you first come across the terminus station of the Golden Valley Light Railway on which narrow gauge trains run on most weekends between April and October and daily during many of the school holidays. This line uses a range of equipment and vehicles acquired from varied industrial sources, mainly local collieries. If trains are running you can use the line to take you to the Railway Museum site at Swanwick Junction or you can continue walking around the end of the line and climb further up the bank through the Midland Railway-Butterley Country Park. The path then continues through the Park with the narrow gauge railway on the left and the standard gauge railway on the right. This 35 acre Country Park was acquired by the railway and the paths and ponds that you can see have been created to make a very pleasant area. A stile at the end of the Country Park leads to a public footpath which crosses both railways. You can then turn left up the footpath a short distance and take

the right fork leading to the railway's Swanwick Junction site. This site contains a large Railway Museum, The Princess Royal Class Locomotive Trust Depot, The Midland Diesel Group Collection, the headquarters of the Golden Valley Light Railway and much more including a Demonstration Signal Box, a Victorian Railwayman's Church, and Brittain Pit Farm Park. All this is well worth exploring.

Crossing Butterley Reservoir

Photo: Robin Stewart-Smith

If the standard gauge railway is running there is the option to travel on this through Butterley station and across Butterley Reservoir to Hammersmith near the western end of Butterley Tunnel (see page 10).

The Midland Railway-Butterley is one of the leading railway preservation sites in the country with its impressive range of locomotives and rolling stock together with other railway infrastructure such as signal boxes and stations, all of which have been built since the railway was taken over in the early 1970s. Virtually everything that you see has been moved from various parts of the country to the railway to bring back its former glory.

Further information is available from Midland Railway-Butterley, Butterley Station, Ripley, Derbyshire DE5 3QZ, by telephone on 01773 570140 or by visiting the web site at www.midlandrailwaycentre.co.uk.

Sims Bridge No12 ▲   ▼ Former Saw Mill at Robin Hood

17

One of only three remaining
original mileposts

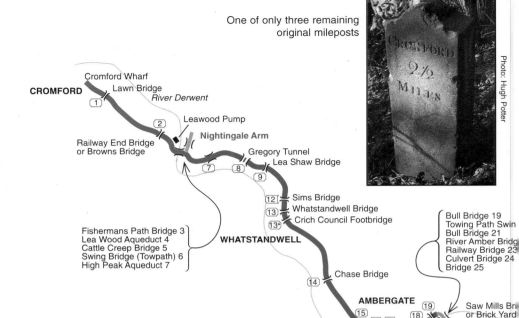

Photo: Hugh Potter

CROMFORD
Cromford Wharf
Lawn Bridge
①
River Derwent

②
Leawood Pump
Nightingale Arm

Railway End Bridge
or Browns Bridge
Gregory Tunnel
⑦ ⑧
Lea Shaw Bridge
⑨

⑫ Sims Bridge
⑬ Whatstandwell Bridge
⑬ᴬ Crich Council Footbridge

Bull Bridge 19
Towing Path Swin
Bull Bridge 21
River Amber Bridg
Railway Bridge 23
Culvert Bridge 24
Bridge 25

Fishermans Path Bridge 3
Lea Wood Aqueduct 4
Cattle Creep Bridge 5
Swing Bridge (Towpath) 6
High Peak Aqueduct 7

WHATSTANDWELL

Chase Bridge
⑭

AMBERGATE ⑲
⑱
Saw Mills Br
or Brick Yard

⑮ ⑯ ⑯ᴬ ⑰
Grattons Bridge
Poysers Bridge
Lime Works Bridge
Hag
Tunnel
⑯
Railway Bridg
⑰

Starvehimvalley or Starvern Bri

Malthou

River Derwent

Cromford Wharf

THE CROMFORD CANAL

Pinxton Wharf

Canal in water

Canal bed intact

Canal bed destroyed

Top Lock Bridge 1
Butterley Co Bridge 2
Ironville Bridge 3
Railway Bridge 4
Fletchers Row Bridge 5
Oakes Tramway Bridge 6
Red Bridge 7

PINXTON

Palmerston Swing Bridge
LNER Bridge ⑬
Colliery Office Bridge ⑫
⑪

Cutts Bridge ⑩
Pinxton Arm ⑨
⑧ Railway Bridge
Pye Bridge

⑦
⑤ ⑥
④ **IRONVILLE**
CODNOR PARK LOCKS 1–7

Amber

Butterley Reservoir

Butterley Park
Reservoir ㉝

Codnor
Park
Reservoir

Hollow Tunnel
RTSHAY ㉜
㉛ Ripley Road Bridge
Hartshay Bridge

Butterley Tunnel

Golden Valley Bridge ㉞ ㉟
Butterley Co Bridge ㊲ Portland Basin
River Erewash

LNER Bridge ㊴
BUTTERLEY CO LOCK 8
㊵ Slaleys Bridge

TOP OF FLIGHT LOCK 1
BOAT DOCK LOCK 2
Lock No 2 Bridge 36
POTTERY LOCK 3
Ironville Bridge 37
SMITH'S LOCK 4
Railway Bridge 38
GAS HOUSE LOCK 5
MARSHALLS LOCK 6
BOTTOM OF FLIGHT LOCK 7

STONEYFORD LOCK 9
Stoneyford Lane Bridge ㊶
STONEYFORD DEEP LOCK 10
STONEYFORD SHALLOW LOCK 11
Bentley Bridge ㊷
Erewash Aqueduct ㊹
VICKER'S LOCK 12
Stoney Lane Bridge ㊺

STRUTT'S LOCK 13 ㊻
Marshalls Bridge ㊼
Beggarlea Bridge
LANGLEY BRIDGE LOCK 14
Nottingham Road Bridge ㊾

LANGLEY MILL

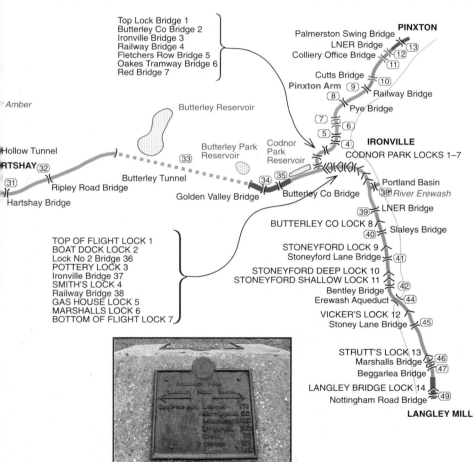
Distance Plaque at Langley Mill

Leawood Pump House

The Leawood Pump

The Cromford Canal Company was formed by Act of Parliament in 1789, and the canal was completed and opened to traffic in 1794. It operated successfully until 1844, which was a particularly dry year and the canal suffered badly from lack of water. This was overcome temporarily by hiring a pump to supplement the water supply by raising water from the River Derwent. In 1845 the Canal Company decided on a permanent solution to this problem, and ordered a pump of their own to be built. The pump we see today was eventually installed in 1849, at a cost of £2900, after some negotiations with the Manchester, Matlock and Midland Joint Railway Company, who were at that time in the process of deciding whether to buy the canal.

Perhaps the most well known feature of the Cromford Canal, the engine house and accompanying boiler house stand between the canal and the river adjacent to Wigwell Aqueduct. The stonework is of a very high standard and looks in as good a condition today as it did over 150 years ago. The engine was built by Graham and Company of Milton Ironworks, Elsecar. It is supplied with steam at 40psi by 2 locomotive type boilers, built by the Midland Railway Company in 1900. The steam passes to a 50 inch diameter steam cylinder, the piston of which has a 9 foot stroke. This is connected via the massive beam which is 33 feet long and weighs 27 tons, to the pump plunger. This is capable of pumping 4 tons of water per stroke and 7 strokes per minute, a total of over 39,000 tons of water per 24 hours. The reason for this apparent over capacity was that the Canal Company was only allowed to pump water from the river from 8.00pm on Saturdays to 8.00pm on Sundays. This was to ensure that the river flow was not depleted for driving the many water mills in the valley at that time. The long summit pound of the canal from Codnor Park to Cromford therefore had to act as a reservoir to enable traffic to keep going all week. At that time, traffic was considerable - 300,000 tons in 1849.

To obtain further details and information on the engine, a visit to the pump house is highly recommended, especially on one of the weekends when the engine is in steam. Although owned by Derbyshire County Council, Leawood Pumphouse is restored, maintained and operated by a group of volunteers, who also look after the Middleton Top Engine on the Cromford and High Peak Railway. More volunteers are always welcomed.

Contact :-   The Leawood Pump House, C/o Countryside Service
                  High Peak Junction, Cromford, Derbyshire Tel: 01629 823204

Cromford Canal Walk : Stage 3
Bullbridge to Cromford Wharf - 6 miles
Plus the Leawood or Nightingale Arm - 1 mile return

This section begins from the towpath just before Bull Bridge No.19. Immediately before the bridge are Bullbridge Cottages on the right, with former Canal Company stables underneath. The bridge is intact but infilled and we must pass up from the towpath and across the road. The Canal Inn is adjacent.

Take the footpath on the other side of the road and pass to the right of Stevenson's Dye Works, part of which is on the canal line.

Bullbridge Cottages

Start of footpath from Bull Bridge No.19 alongside Stevenson's Dye Works

When this path turns sharp right, look straight on along Stevenson's yard. The canal passed straight through here and there is a steel pipe bridge marked "Caution 10' 6" Clearance". This is in its original position and crosses the infilled canal line.

Pipe bridge indicates canal line through Stevenson's yard

Steps through the wood on the diversion

From this point we must make an extensive diversion via the public footpath round Stevenson's and Transco's works. Turn right here to follow the path which climbs steeply uphill. After a path joins from the right, we continue ahead for a short distance then turn sharp right at the Cromford Canal Footpath sign, and up a long flight of steps which come as quite a surprise in the middle of a wood.

At the top follow the path to a stone stile. Climb over and turn left to follow the stone wall. The path continues along the hedge side beyond the wall and then by a chain link fence, which borders the Transco plant. This part is very undulating but the path is apparent and sometimes mown. Follow to the right of the fence and descend, over a stile and on down to once again rejoin the canal.

There is now water in the channel and a good towpath on the left bank. Carry on under a water

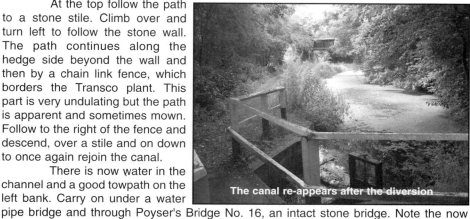
The canal re-appears after the diversion

pipe bridge and through Poyser's Bridge No. 16, an intact stone bridge. Note the now fading painted bridge number.

From now on, there is a good towpath which is easily followed through to Cromford.

We pass Grattons Bridge No. 15, and two stone cottages, then a little way to Chase Bridge No. 14, another intact stone arch.

A very pleasant stretch to Whatstandwell follows. Pass under Crich Council Footbridge No. 13a, which is adjacent to Whatstandwell railway station. Shortly then to Whatstandwell Bridge No. 13, where there is a stone house on the towpath side built over the railway tunnel. The house

Poyser's Bridge No. 16

opposite is on a former wharf immediately before the bridge. The Derwent Hotel is just down the hill alongside the A6.

The attractive scenery of the Derwent Valley is now becoming apparent.

Sims Bridge No. 12 follows, which now has a modern steel deck on the old stone abutments.

Whatstandwell Bridge No. 13

Former Sawmill at Robin Hood

Following this we pass over a culvert which still carries it's original No. 10 bridge plate on the towpath wall, opposite a former stone sawmill converted into an attractive house, at Robin Hood.

A further 100 yards on is a concrete 2½ mile post on the towpath. Opposite, somewhat hidden, an original milestone is still in place showing 2½ miles to Cromford.

Next is Lea Shaw Bridge No. 9 with worn stone steps adjacent which lead up to an interesting group of old stone buildings.

We then reach Gregory Widehole, which is followed by the short Gregory Tunnel. Walk through on the towpath.

The modern concrete 2 mile post is just beyond. Shortly after this is another interesting feature, the iron trough aqueduct (Bridge No. 7) which carries the canal over the railway. Notice the railway tunnel adjacent to the aqueduct on the offside.

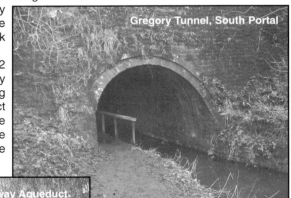

Gregory Tunnel, South Portal

Railway Aqueduct.

Follow the towpath round a right hand bend to a junction with the Leawood or Nightingale Arm, which turns off to the right. At the junction the towpath crosses from left to right via Swingbridge No. 6.

If you wish to explore the arm, turn right after passing over the swingbridge. See next page.

To continue on the main line, turn to page 26.

The Leawood or Nightingale Branch

This half mile branch was built in 1800 by Peter Nightingale (great uncle of the famous Florence).

Aqueduct Cottage on the right of the junction has now sadly fallen into disrepair and is almost lost in the foliage.

The start of the arm is marked by a stone built narrows, the recesses for the stop gate being clearly visible.

At first the towpath traverses a narrow strip of land between the River

Junction with Leawood Branch

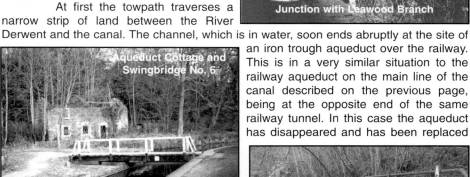

Aqueduct Cottage and Swingbridge No. 6

Derwent and the canal. The channel, which is in water, soon ends abruptly at the site of an iron trough aqueduct over the railway. This is in a very similar situation to the railway aqueduct on the main line of the canal described on the previous page, being at the opposite end of the same railway tunnel. In this case the aqueduct has disappeared and has been replaced

Site of Railway Aqueduct

by a steel footbridge to carry the towpath over the railway.

Beyond here the canal bed is dry but intact. The towpath makes a pleasant walk through Lea Wood to the wharf at the terminus. Just before the wharf, there is a small stone building on the towpath, note that this incorporates a stone gatepost with the familiar grooves worn by horseboat towlines. The wharfinger's stone cottage is intact and has been extended to make an attractive private residence. On the edge of the wharf, the remains of a wooden crane stump with an iron turntable can be clearly seen.

Leawood Wharf

The canal now terminates at this wharf but originally continued into Lea Bridge, which is reached along the track straight ahead. The original terminus was to the left of this track and is now occupied by the factory shop car park at John Smedley's Lea Mills.

To resume our walk on the main line of the canal towards Cromford, turn left after crossing Swingbridge No. 6 to follow the towpath across Wigwell or Leawood Aqueduct.

This elegant structure crosses the River Derwent in a single span and is perhaps best seen from below to appreciate the fine lines.

To do this, one needs to scramble down the bank to river level on the south side.

Wigwell Aqueduct from below

Continuing on the towpath over the aqueduct, the Leawood Pumphouse is on the right between canal and river. This impressive stone building contains a large beam engine which was used to pump water up from the River Derwent to feed the canal.

Wigwell Aqueduct and Leawood Pumphouse

It is still in working order and is steamed by enthusiasts on several weekends in the summer.

[*See page 21 for details*].

Almost opposite this is the former transhipment warehouse, which marks the start of the Cromford and High Peak Railway. This was built to connect the Cromford Canal over the Derbyshire hills to the Peak Forest Canal at Whaley Bridge, via a series of steep rope-worked inclines. The line has now been converted into a walking and cycle way.

The enthusiast will no doubt wish to explore this fascinating link separately.

Transhipment Warehouse

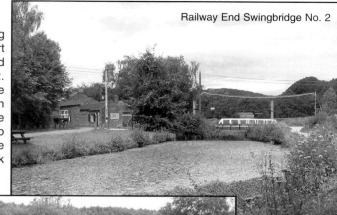
Railway End Swingbridge No. 2

Continue along the towpath a short distance to Railway End Swingbridge No. 2. Across this bridge are the High Peak Junction Workshops and the bottom of the Sheep Pasture Incline of the Cromford and High Peak Railway .

High Peak Junction

Here there are toilets, a useful information centre and a shop selling a wide range of interesting items as well as some refreshments. This is also the office of the Canal Ranger Service run by Derbyshire County Council.

Re-join the towpath and continue along this pleasant stretch to pass the stone arched Lawn Bridge No. 1, then shortly reach Cromford Wharf.

This is a classic canal terminus in an idyllic setting in the Derwent Valley adjacent to Cromford Meadows. Arkwright's world famous cotton mill is across the road.

Here the canal widens and divides into two arms with two interesting old stone warehouses each with a canopy over the canal.

Cromford Wharf is a popular spot with a large pay and display car park and public toilets.

Approaching Cromford Wharf

Cromford Village

Cromford itself is an interesting and historic place in the Derwent Valley which is perhaps most famous for the fact that Richard Arkwright built the world's first successful water driven cotton mill here in 1771. It is an ideal location for water mills having an abundant water supply. A visit to the Arkwright Society's shops in the mill complex opposite the wharf is highly recommended.

The Courtyard at Arkwright's Mill now incorporating various shops

Cromford Station

To the right from the wharf is the ancient stone bridge over the River Derwent with ruins of the bridge chapel. Continuing in this direction, we come to Cromford railway station with its delightful original buildings dating from 1849.

Turning the opposite way, and across the other side of the A6, is the centre of the village. Passing through the market place, we come to the mill pond with the Boat Inn nearby and at the opposite end a working waterwheel which originally turned a flour mill. Alongside the pond is the Scarthin book shop, a bibliophile's paradise which certainly should not be missed. There is an excellent Guide to Cromford which is published by this fine establishment.

Waterwheel

The mill pond

The Arkwright Society

by Christopher Charlton

The Derwent Valley has been called the Cradle of the Industrial Revolution, its international significance being recognised by UNESCO in December 2001 when part of the valley, between Matlock Bath and Derby, was inscribed as a World Heritage Site. The essential first step towards a place in world history was taken when Richard Arkwright

The wharfside building to be renovated by the Arkwright Society

built the first successful water powered cotton spinning mill at Cromford in 1771. The mill remains a monument to his extraordinary genius. At the same time, he developed Cromford into one of the first industrial villages, including workers cottages, market place and lock up.

The Arkwright Society, based at Cromford Mill, grew out of the Arkwright Festival which in 1971 commemorated the two hundredth anniversary of Arkwright's arrival. It is a registered charity and an amenity society registered with the Civic Trust.

The Society purchased the Cromford Mill site in 1979 and began the difficult task of restoring this important industrial complex. The work has included a massive decontamination programme, clearing the site of chemicals which were the legacy of more than fifty years as a colour works, manufacturing colour pigments for paints and dyes.

Visitor facilities at Cromford Mill include an exhibition and shops selling books, gifts, cards and re-cycled paper products in addition to a wholefood restaurant providing a wide range of delicious hot meals and cakes.

Renovation work is currently being carried out on the canal side wharf building which, on its completion in March 2004, will house an exhibition by George Jones and Hugh Potter on the 1st floor. The exhibition will provide a photographic history of the canal in addition to presenting a series of historical walks. A café supplying a range of home made hot snacks and sandwiches will also be opening on the ground floor.

Joining the Arkwright Society will help to support the restoration and on going maintenance of this internationally significant project. Volunteers are always needed to help with the practical daily tasks as well as to help organise many local projects.

Contact the Society at Cromford Mill, Mill Lane, Cromford, Derbyshire DE4 3RQ
Tel: 01629 823256 e mail: info@cromfordmill.co.uk

The Pinxton Branch

The Pinxton Branch leaves the main line of the Cromford Canal at Ironville, adjacent to the site of Top of Flight Lock No.1. This 2¼ mile branch ran on one level from Ironville through Pye Bridge to Pinxton Wharf.

Top Lock Bridge No. 1

As mentioned earlier in this guide, the top lock was removed in the 1980s and the level of Codnor Park reservoir lowered as part of an ill-conceived flood relief scheme. This means that Top Lock Bridge No.1, a fine intact stone arch over the entrance to the arm, now stands in isolation.

The towpath at the start of the branch was on the right through this bridge but this is now very overgrown. The better path now starts on the left hand side, passing along the eastern end of the Codnor Park Reservoir, on the top of the retaining wall. This separates the reservoir on the left from the now infilled Pinxton Branch on the right.

On reaching the north east corner of the reservoir, the Pinxton Branch turns sharply to the right and passes under Butterley Company Bridge No.2 which nowadays has a modern footbridge deck on the old abutments.

Butterley Company Bridge No. 2

Ironville Church and Church Bridge No. 3

The path now lies in the infilled canal bed, and continues with an old stone towpath wall on the right. A vehicle access joins the canal line and leads to the back of Ironville Village Hall, where there is a car park on the former canal bed.

We then pass close to the rear of Ironville Church and vicarage with the cemetery on the left and under Ironville or Church Bridge No. 3. This was originally a stone arch bridge but is now a modern flat-decked structure, strengthened underneath with a concrete buttress.

Looking back at Ironville Church and Church Bridge No. 3

Railway Bridge No. 4

Photo: Hugh Potter

Beyond here the canal line is grassed over and swings to the left passing the last of the houses in Ironville and under the Railway Bridge No. 4. This is the Butterley Branch Railway which has been taken over by the Midland Railway Centre. Steam trains can quite often be seen on this bridge.

More details of the Midland Railway Centre's activities are given on page 16

The good path continues after the railway bridge on the right hand side of the infilled canal. About 200 yards further on, a road crosses the canal line at a low level between stone walls. This is the site of Fletchers Row Bridge No. 5. There is a modern concrete $1/2$ mile post still in situ just beyond here.

The next section is a pleasant walk along a landscaped section where a large number of small trees have been planted. The path passes through the centre of these, but there is no sign of the canal. Oakes Tramway Bridge No. 6 and Red Bridge No. 7 were along this length but have disappeared completely. The tree lined section continues to the Main Road Bridge No. 8 at Pye Bridge. This bridge is infilled but intact, now with a flat deck and steel railings. The old canalside cottages remain adjacent to here.

Cross over the road and continue along the towpath which is now on the right of a very short length of canal still in water, with the old stone wall remaining on the right.

Cottages at Pye Bridge No. 8

The infilled channel then resumes and the path again passes through a great many young trees planted on the landscaped canal. As with many infilled canals, drainage is a problem here and the path can be very muddy in wet weather.

We shortly come to Railway Bridge No. 9. This is a twin-arched blue brick

Railway Bridge No. 9

structure which carries the main Erewash Valley railway over the canal line.

Immediately after this bridge we encounter the former Smotherfly opencast coal site, a major obstacle to the canal. This area has recently been opencast mined, which has greatly altered the lie of the land. The River Erewash has been diverted and the canal line completely obliterated. To carry on with the walk to Pinxton we must follow an extensive diversion for about a mile:

Do not pass under the railway bridge, but turn sharp left on to a footpath immediately before it. Follow this path as it crosses the remains of a former railway embankment, then continue on the path with the main line railway on your right. The path is fenced off from the adjacent fields on the left. After approx. $1/2$ mile pass through the remains of a stile and turn right on to a track and walk under the main line railway.

Main Line Railway Bridge on Diversion

Then follow this track straight ahead for some 500 yards and through a branch railway bridge. Just beyond this bridge we can again see the opencast area and the diverted River Erewash.

Branch Railway Bridge

Turn immediately left to cross a small wooden bridge over a stream to follow a footpath. This runs closely along the right hand side of the railway for another 500 yards, then turns sharp right, away from the railway and alongside a commercial vehicle scrapyard for a short distance.

We emerge through a stile (dismantled) and turn right, away from the scrapyard gates along a track. This shortly passes through two gates and we then arrive beside some recognisable canal!

The channel is in water here which runs over a weir at this end. The towpath has been widened into a track which is the access road to the scrapyard. This has meant that the canal is narrower than originally built, but it is full of water!

The track then leaves to the right, and the towpath continues

Canal in water approaching Pinxton

ahead alongside the water. There is a low level wooden footbridge across the canal. This has been built on the original stone abutments of Palmerston Swingbridge No. 13.

Looking back at the Boat Inn - Pinxton

We then shortly come to a small canalside terrace followed by the Boat Inn. This is an old canal pub which is still largely unaltered since the boats used to tie here.

There is then a small gate on the towpath and another low level footbridge across the canal.

Towpath Gate

Footbridge just before Pinxton Wharf

The former wharf and terminal basin at Pinxton is just beyond and is a large area of water which has been restored by Derbyshire CC and Broxtowe District Council. It provides a pleasant landscaped area with seats etc. and is also a thriving fishery.

Pinxton Wharf

The railway is adjacent and we cross over the level crossing to give access to the village and buses if required. The main road through Pinxton is called Wharf Road, which is perhaps indicative of the importance of the canal in times past.

Return Transport

By Bus:

There is a generally good bus service in this area. In all cases, phone the bus enquiry number: **0870 608 2608**

Ironville (King William St.) to Langley Mill	Change at Eastwood or Ripley
Bullbridge to Ironville	Change at Ripley or Alfreton
Cromford to Bullbridge	Change at Ambergate
Pinxton to Ironville	Direct

All these services apply in either direction and are normally at least once an hour. The number above will give full up to date details.

By Train:

Please use the national rail enquiry number: **08457 484950**

Langley Mill station is about 10 minutes walk from the canal on the main A608 road through Langley Mill.

There are no rail services at Ironville, Pinxton or Bullbridge.

Ambergate station is near the junction of the A610 with the A6. To reach the canal, walk north on the A6 for 200 yards and turn right up Chase Road and pass under the railway to join the canal at Poyser's Bridge No.16.

Whatstandwell station is close by the canal alongside the A6. There is direct access from the station to the towpath via the footbridge.

Cromford station is reached from the wharf by turning right from the wharf entrance and over the river bridge. Keep right after the bridge and follow the road for 300 yards. The station is up a road to the left.

The three last have car parking facilities.

Cromford to Langley Mill or vice versa takes about 1 hr 45 mins, changing at Derby and Nottingham.

Cromford to Whatstandwell or Ambergate takes only a few minutes.

Again use the above number for full details.

By Car:

In addition to the station car parks above, convenient car parking places near the canal are as follows:-

Langley Mill	Linkmel Road near the Great Northern Basin
Ironville	Car park on the canal line near Codnor Park Reservoir (Page 7)
Pinxton	On the approach to the Boat Inn beyond the Basin
Lower Hartshay	At the closed end of the former main Ripley road by the Gate Inn
Bullbridge	On the street by the Canal Inn
Whatstandwell	Small car park on the canal side by Whatstandwell Bridge No. 13
High Peak Junction	Car park across the river from the canal on Lea Road
Cromford	Large car park at the Wharf (Pay and Display) or on Cromford Meadows